HADES

THE ONLY OLYMPIAN GOD WHO DIDN'T LIVE ON MOUNT OLYMPUS

GREEK MYTHOLOGY FOR KIDS
CHILDREN'S GREEK & ROMAN BOOKS

AF485168

Speedy Publishing LLC

40 E. Main St. #1156

Newark, DE 19711

www.speedypublishing.com

Copyright 2017

All Rights reserved. No part of this book may be reproduced or used in any way or form or by any means whether electronic or mechanical, this means that you cannot record or photocopy any material ideas or tips that are provided in this book.

In this book, we're going to talk about the Greek god Hades. So, let's get right to it!

Who Is Hades?

Hades is the mythological Greek god who ruled the location that we describe today as hell. The Romans called him "Pluto." In Greek mythology, the underworld was a place of shadows that was located under the Earth. It was the last resting place for dead souls. Because most humans are scared of death, Hades was feared and the Greek writer Homer described Hades as "monstrous." The word "hades" was also used for the place where the god Hades lived.

TITAN

HOW DID HE BECOME THE RULER OF THE UNDERWORLD?

The gods of Olympus weren't the first Greek gods. The Titans came before them and the Giants, a race known for their immense strength, also had control over the skies and the seas before the Olympians. Both the Titans and the Giants were eventually overthrown by the Olympians and three Greek gods from Mount Olympus came into power.

These gods were the sons of Titan parents named Cronus, who was king, and Rhea, who was queen. The three brothers were:

- ZEUS, the god who ruled the sky and who ruled all the Olympian gods

ZEUS

POSEIDON

- Poseidon, the god who ruled the seas

- Hades, the god who ruled the underworld

At the beginning, Hades wasn't happy that he had drawn the lot of the underworld for his domain. However, Zeus told him that eventually everyone would die so they would all be subjects of Hades! This reasoning seemed to appease him.

HADES

ades didn't appear in as many myths as the other gods and goddesses, possibly because he was so feared. In fact, the Greek people didn't even like to mention him by name so they used other terms, such as Eubuleus, for him. Another common name they used for him was Plouton, which translates to "lord of riches."

Sometimes to appease him they would make sacrificial offerings. Blood from the offerings would flow down into the ground and supposedly to the underworld so that Hades would receive their homage.

MYTHICAL GATEWAY TO HADES

Although Hades was considered to be one of the dozen most important gods, he didn't reside on Mount Olympus. In fact, he was the only god that didn't live there. Instead, his dark, shadowy palace lay under the Earth.

THE STORY OF THE BIRTH OF HADES

When Rhea gave birth to Hades, his father Cronus swallowed him up. The reason was that there had been a foretelling that Hades would defeat his father. Cronus swallowed him to prevent that from happening. Zeus, who was younger than Hades, ended up saving him.

RHEA

HEPHAESTUS

THE HELMET THAT MADE HIM INVISIBLE

The god of metalworking, Hephaistos, made a special helmet for Hades. When an individual wore the helmet it made him or her invisible. In the epic poem The Iliad, the Greek writer Homer told the story that the goddess Athena borrowed the helmet.

She made herself invisible when she did battle with her rival half-brother Ares during the Trojan War. Perseus, the great Greek warrior, borrowed the helmet to do battle with the female monster Medusa who had snakes for hair. He killed her and cut off her head!

ATHENA

CHARON WITH BOAT TRAVELING IN STYX SEA

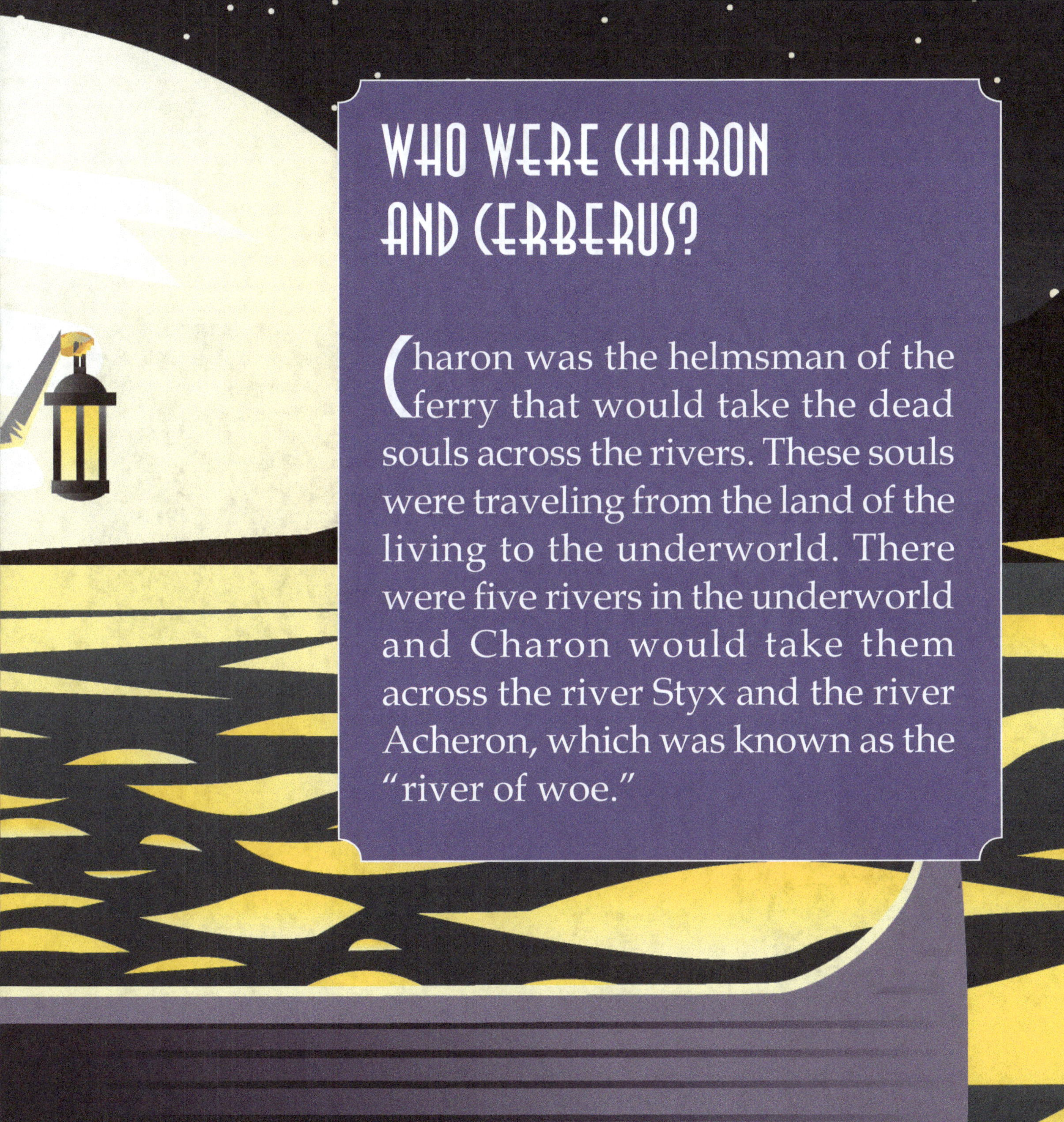

WHO WERE CHARON AND CERBERUS?

Charon was the helmsman of the ferry that would take the dead souls across the rivers. These souls were traveling from the land of the living to the underworld. There were five rivers in the underworld and Charon would take them across the river Styx and the river Acheron, which was known as the "river of woe."

If the dead person didn't pay a coin to Charon for his payment, the person would be abandoned on the shore where he or she would wander aimlessly for 100 years.

THE TWO SIDES OF AN ANCIENT GREEK GOLD COIN

In the real world, the Greeks would place a coin in the mouths of their loved ones before they were buried so they could easily pay the toll when they got to the underworld.

Hades also had a special gigantic, fierce dog to help him. The name of this dog was Cerberus and he had three heads with sharp teeth. His duty was to guard the underworld entrance. The living were not allowed inside and the dead were not allowed to escape.

CERBERUS

DEMETER

THE "LOVE STORY" OF HADES AND PERSEPHONE

Zeus, the god of the sky, and Demeter, the goddess of agriculture, had a beautiful daughter named Persephone. Many gods tried to win the hand of the innocent Persephone, but her mother Demeter worked hard to keep her away from the gods. Hades was lonely down in the underworld by himself and he began to envision Persephone as his wife.

At that time on Earth, it was an eternal springtime. Persephone was out enjoying the sunshine and smelling the beautiful flowers when Hades thundered through with his chariot driven by four deathly black horses. He kidnapped the gorgeous Persephone and dragged her down to the underworld with him.

When Demeter went to look for her daughter, she couldn't find her anywhere. She went in search all over the Earth for nine full days and nights. She was so distraught that she destroyed crops and livestock everywhere she went. Her grief was so powerful that she threatened to destroy the Earth and all the mortals living there if her daughter wasn't found.

Of course, Zeus knew that his brother had wanted his daughter Persephone all along, but he didn't tell Demeter where she was. Rhea, who was the mother of Zeus and Hades was in charge of the negotiations. Persephone would be allowed to return to her mother for six months of the year and during those months flowers would bloom and fruits would ripen.

THE RETURN OF PERSPEPHONE

PERSPEPHONE

However, in the fall and winter, Persephone would have to return to her husband in the underworld. Then, the Earth would become cold and barren to show her mother's grief as she missed her daughter.

HOW WAS HADES DEPICTED?

In Greek art, Hades is shown with a beard. He is usually wearing his helmet or a crown. He holds a pitchfork with only two prongs compared to Poseidon's pitchfork, which has three prongs. He is sometimes holding a drinking vessel. Cerberus is often at his feet or by his side.

In some depictions he is shown driving a chariot that is pulled by four, black-as-night horses. At times, his wife Persephone is at his side as he sits on a throne made of ebony. In some artistic renderings, he has a cornucopia to show the wealth of vegetables that grow from the ground.

THE PLACE OF HADES

Hades was also the term for the actual locations within the underworld. Not all these locations were bad. Some were more like heaven than hell. When they arrived at the gates, dead souls were judged by the actions they had taken when they were alive. There were three judges who had lived honorably so they were in a position to determine whether others had done the same.

Those who had lived well and had done good deeds in their lives were first taken to the Lethe River. There they would drink and the water would help them to forget anything bad that had happened to them in their lives. After that, they were brought to the beautiful Elysian Fields. However, those who had done bad deeds throughout their lives were brought to Tartarus, the very lowest level of the underworld.

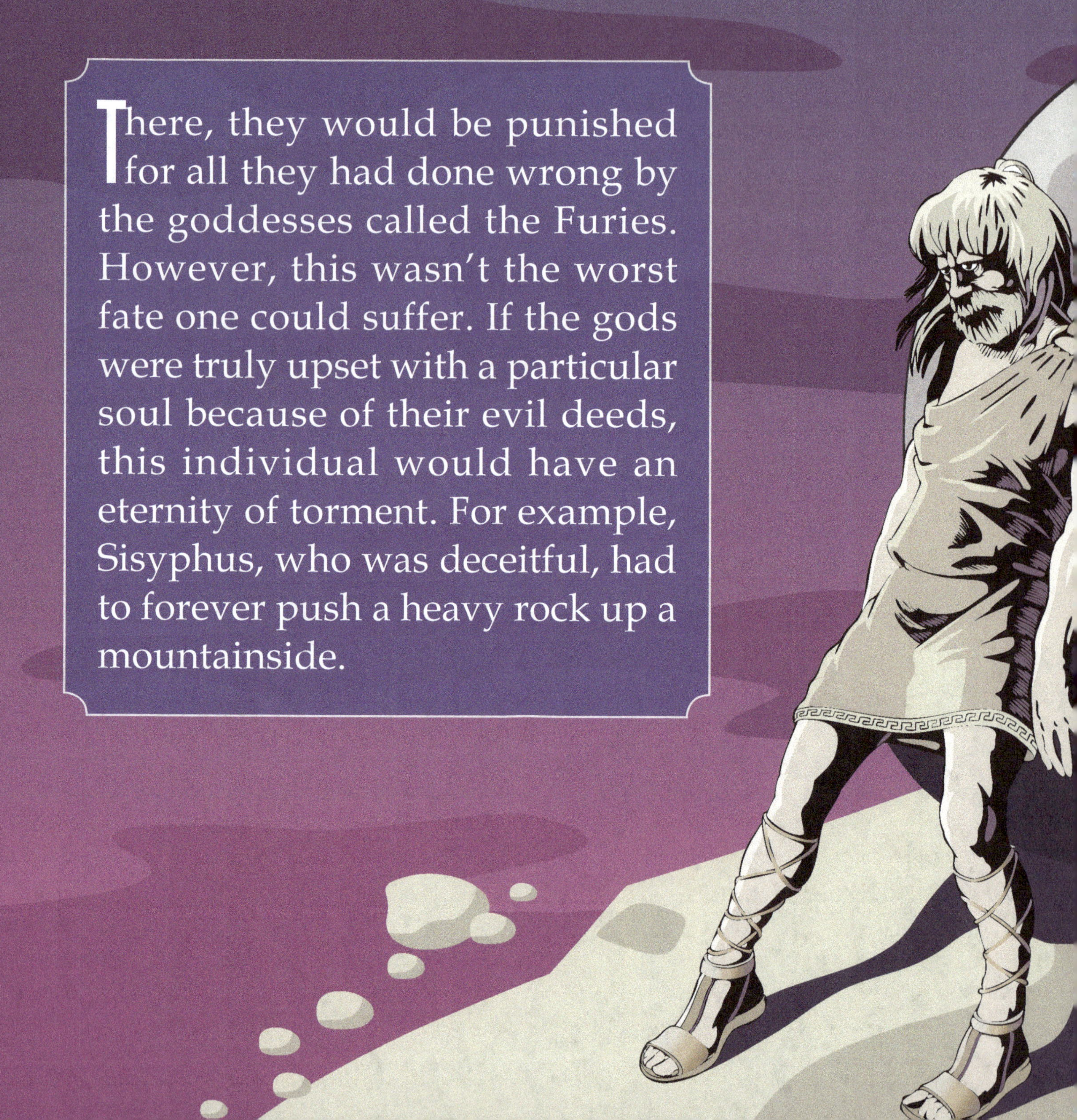

There, they would be punished for all they had done wrong by the goddesses called the Furies. However, this wasn't the worst fate one could suffer. If the gods were truly upset with a particular soul because of their evil deeds, this individual would have an eternity of torment. For example, Sisyphus, who was deceitful, had to forever push a heavy rock up a mountainside.

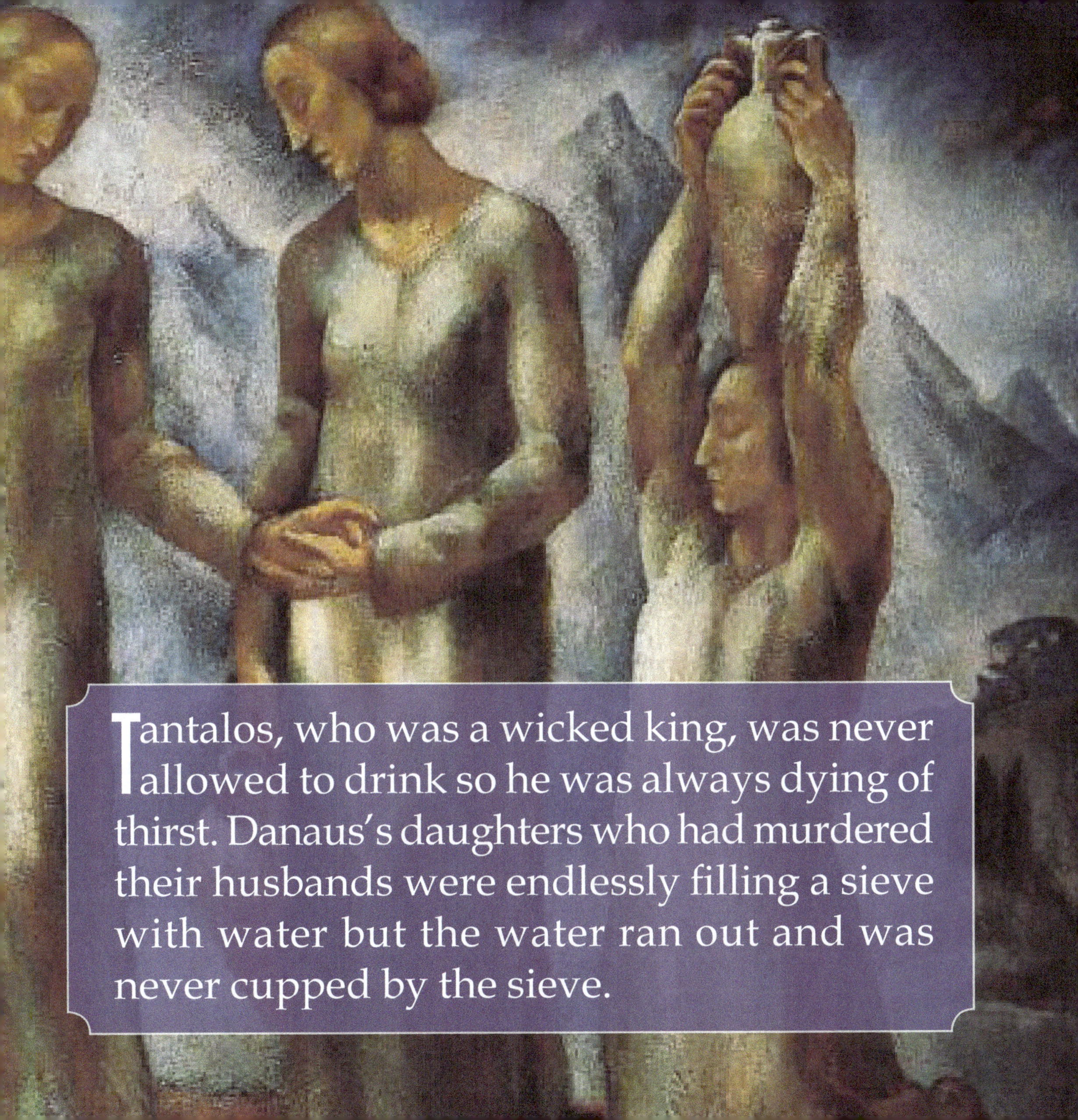

Tantalos, who was a wicked king, was never allowed to drink so he was always dying of thirst. Danaus's daughters who had murdered their husbands were endlessly filling a sieve with water but the water ran out and was never cupped by the sieve.

HADES – GREEK GOD OF THE DEAD AND KING OF THE UNDERWORLD

Zeus, Poseidon, and Hades were brothers. When the Olympians won the battle for the rule of the Earth and the heavens, the brothers decided to draw lots to see who would rule which location. Hades drew the underworld, his brother Zeus was given the sky, and Poseidon was given the seas. Hades wasn't pleased but Zeus convinced him that everyone would eventually live in the underworld so Hades would have a huge kingdom.

Hades was lonely in the underworld and no one wanted to marry him so he kidnapped the beautiful Persephone for his bride. She was forever doomed to live in the underworld with him. The eternal springtime of Earth became the four seasons because of her mother Demeter's grief.

Awesome! Now that you've read about the Greek god Hades, you may want to read about another god and a goddess in the Baby Professor book *Ares vs. Athena: Who Won the Battle? Mythology Books for Kids.*

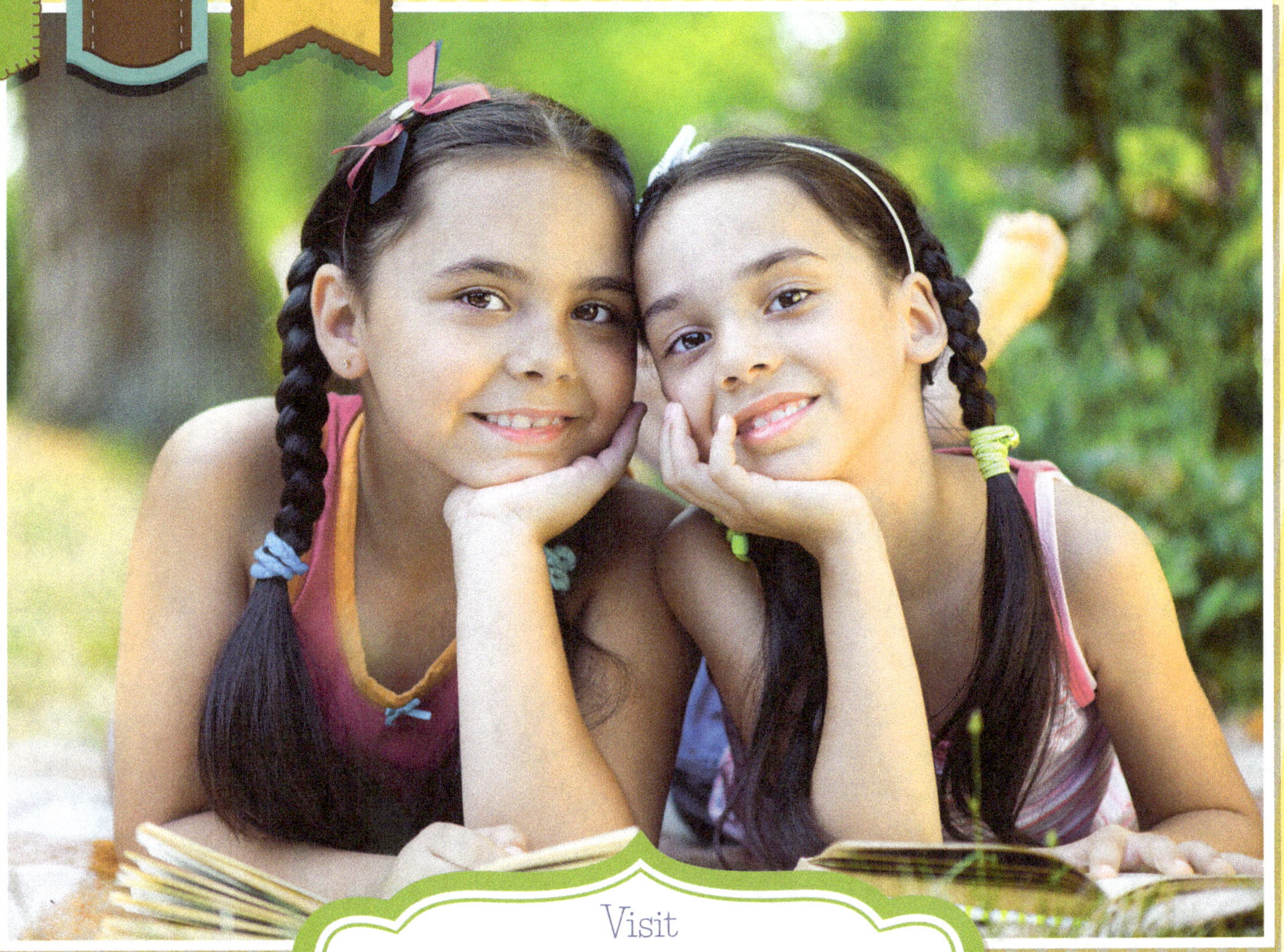

Visit

www.BabyProfessorBooks.com

to download Free Baby Professor eBooks
and view our catalog of new and exciting
Children's Books

www.ingramcontent.com/pod-product-compliance
Lightning Source LLC
Chambersburg PA
CBHW060130120726
48003CB00009B/2834